FLOWERS

DAISIES

John F. Prevost
ABDO & Daughters

Published by Abdo & Daughters, 4940 Viking Drive, Suite 622, Edina, Minnesota 55435.

Copyright © 1996 by Abdo Consulting Group, Inc., Pentagon Tower, P.O. Box 36036, Minneapolis, Minnesota 55435 USA. International copyrights reserved in all countries. No part of this book may be reproduced in any form without written permission from the publisher.

Printed in the United States.

Cover Photo credits: Peter Arnold, Inc.
Interior Photo credits: Peter Arnold, Inc.

Edited by Bob Italia

Library of Congress Cataloging-in-Publication Data

Prevost, John F.
      Daisies / John F. Prevost.
      p. cm. -- (Flowers)
      Includes index.
      Summary: Describes the structure of and growing conditions for this popular flower and includes information about its various species and pests and diseases that affect it.
      ISBN 1-56239-608-0
      1. Daisies--Juvenile literature. [1. Daisies.] I. Title. II. Series: Prevost, John F. Flowers
      QK495.C74P735 1996
      583' .55--dc20
                                           96-11452
                                                CIP
                                              AC

Contents

Daisies and Family

Daisies are a group of popular **annual** and **perennial** plants. Their flowers are often yellow centered with white rays, like the Shasta or oxeye daisies. Or they may grow in several different colors, like the painted daisy.

Daisy plants are easily started from seeds. Annual daisies will grow, bloom, and seed for only one season. Many will reseed themselves each year. Perennial daisies will live many years, growing back each spring.

All daisies are part of the aster and daisy family. The aster and daisy family is the second largest plant family. It has more than 15,000 types of flowers, including chrysanthemums, sunflowers, and zinnias.

Opposite page: A field filled with oxeye daisies.

Roots, Soil, and Water

Daisies pull water from the ground with their roots. Water contains **minerals** and other **nutrients** the plant uses for food. Roots also help hold the plant upright and keep it from falling over.

Daisies grow in different soil types. Some grow best in dry, sandy soil. Others like wet, fertile soil. Daisies may have special roots. Some form **tubers** and help the plant store food for the next season. Other daisy plants spread from **rhizomes**.

Roots hold the daisy upright.

Stems, Leaves, and Sunlight

The stems and leaves are the parts of the daisy that grow above ground. Sunlight is important to every green plant. Plants use sunlight to change water, **nutrients,** and air into food and **oxygen.** This process is called **photosynthesis.**

The stems support the leaves and allow them to capture sunlight. Stems also connect the leaves to the roots. They allow water and nutrients collected by the roots to reach the leaves. Food made by the leaves then travels to the roots.

Photosynthesis

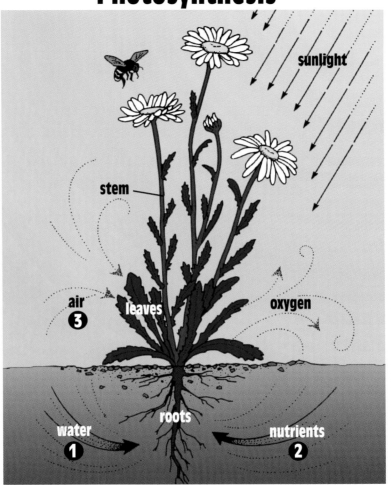

Ground water (1) and nutrients (2) travel through the roots and stems and into the leaves where air (3) is drawn in. Then the plant uses sunlight to change these three elements into food and oxygen.

Flowers

Daisies are grown in many gardens. They are popular and beautiful flowers. A daisy **flower head** is made up of many small flowers held together. The center or **disk** flowers are the fertile flowers; they make seeds. The **rays** are often **infertile** flowers.

The small flowers that are in the flower head have two main parts: the **stamen** and the **pistil**. The stamen makes the **pollen** that the insects carry to other daisies. The pollen **fertilizes ovules** in the pistil. These ovules become seeds.

The name "daisy" comes from the Old English description, "day's eye." The center or disk is often yellow. The rays surrounding the disk are often white. Some types have different colored disks and rays.

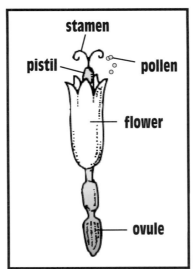

The daisy flower head is made of many small flowers. Each small flower has a stamen that fertilizes the pistil's ovule.

11

Seeds

Each tiny flower in the **flower head's disk** makes one seed. The seeds are held tightly within the flower head until they become ripe. Some seed types are blown in the wind. Others fall to the ground.

Daisies grow flowers to make seeds. Each seed contains a plant **embryo.** There is enough food within the seed to give the tiny plant a chance to grow.

Many people plant seeds to start their daisies. **Perennial** daisies may be started by seed or root divisions. Root divisions are clumps of roots that will grow new daisies when replanted.

disk

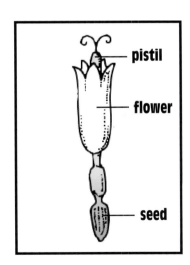

pistil

flower

seed

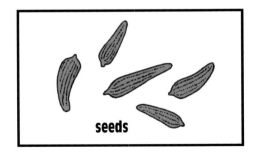

seeds

After the pistil's ovule is fertilized, it becomes a seed. Each seed contains a tiny embryo, which will grow into a daisy plant.

Insects and Other Friends

Some insects are good for plants. Daisies grow flowers to attract **pollinating** insects. The insects are rewarded with a small meal of **nectar** in the **flower head**. Pollen sticks to bees, butterflies, and other insects that carry pollen from flower to flower. This is how flowers are **fertilized.**

Many **predatory** insects live on daisy plants. Ladybugs, lacewings, and wasps help the plant by eating insect **pests**. Spiders also live on the leaves and stems. They do not harm the plant, but eat its enemies.

Ladybugs eat insect pests.

Many types of insects live on daisy plants.

Pests and Diseases

Some insects are harmful to plants. These are known as **pests**. **Aphids** may be a problem in some gardens. Often, **predatory** insects and spiders will control these pests.

Caterpillars may eat some daisies, but are not always pests. Some people grow wildflower and butterfly gardens to feed caterpillars. The caterpillars become butterflies or moths.

Healthy daisy plants can fight **disease**. But when daisies are planted in the wrong areas, they become weak. Diseases will attack weakened daisies. **Chemicals** are substances used to control these diseases.

Healthy daisies can cover an entire field.

Varieties

Daisies have their own large plant family. Zinnias, sunflowers, chrysanthemums, asters, and all daisy **varieties** are part of the daisy family.

Daisy plants may be 10 to 12 inches (25 to 30 cm) or 3 to 5 feet (1 to 1.5 meters) tall. The flowers are often white, blue, or red. The **disk** can be yellow, brown, or black.

Opposite page:
Daisy plants can have
white, blue, or red flowers.

Daisies and the Plant Kingdom

The plant kingdom is divided into several groups, including flowering plants, fungi, plants with bare seeds, and ferns.

 Flowering plants grow flowers to make seeds. These seeds often grow inside protective ovaries or fruit.

 Fungi are plants without leaves, flowers, or green coloring, and cannot make their own food. They include mushrooms, molds, and yeast.

 Plants with bare seeds (such as evergreens and conifers) do not grow flowers. Their seeds grow unprotected, often on the scale of a cone.

 Ferns are plants with roots, stems, and leaves. They do not grow flowers or seeds.

There are two groups of flowering plants: monocots (MAH-no-cots) and dicots (DIE-cots). Monocots have seedlings with one leaf. Dicots have seedlings with two leaves.

The aster and daisy family is one type of dicot. All daisy varieties are part of the aster and daisy family.

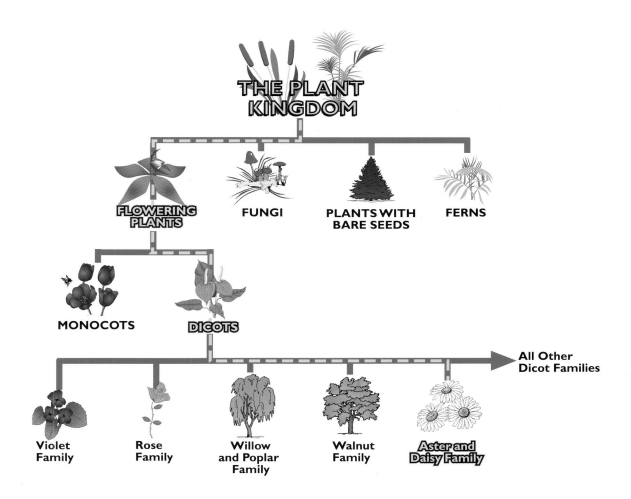

THE PLANT KINGDOM

FLOWERING PLANTS

FUNGI

PLANTS WITH BARE SEEDS

FERNS

MONOCOTS

DICOTS

All Other Dicot Families

Violet Family

Rose Family

Willow and Poplar Family

Walnut Family

Aster and Daisy Family

21

Glossary

annual (ANN-yoo-ull) - A plant that grows from a seed and matures and dies in a single season.

aphid (AY-fid) - A small insect that sucks the sap from plant leaves and stems.

blossom (BLAH-sum) - The flower of a plant.

chemical (KEM-ma-kull) - A substance used to create a reaction or process.

disease (DUH-zees) - A condition of an animal or plant that impairs performance.

disk- The center part of the daisy flower head.

embryo (EM-bree-oh) - An early stage of plant growth, before sprouting from a seed.

fertilize (FUR-tuh-lies) - To develop the ovule into a seed.

flower head - Many small daisy flowers held together.

infertile- Not able to reproduce.

mineral - Any substance that is not a plant, animal, or another living thing.

nectar- A sweet fluid found in some flowers.

nutrient (NEW-tree-ent) - Substances that help a plant grow and keep it healthy.

ovule (AH-vule) - A seed before it is fertilized by pollen.

oxygen (OX-ih-jen) - A gas without color, taste, or odor found in air and water.

perennial (purr-EN-ee-ull) - A plant that lives for three or more years.

pest - A harmful or destructive insect.

petal (PET-ull) - One of several leaves that protect the center of a flower.

photosynthesis (foe-toe-SIN-thuh-sis) - The use of sunlight to make food.

pistil (PIS-tull) - The female (seed-making) flower part.

pollen - A yellow powder that fertilizes flowers.

pollinate (PAHL-ih-nate) - To fertilize a flower with pollen.

predator (PRED-uh-tore) - An animal that eats other animals.

rays - The flowers that surround the daisy's disk.

rhizome (RYE-zome) - An underground stem with roots.

stamen (STAY-men) - The male flower part (the flower part that makes pollen).

tuber (TOO-bur) - The thick part of a root used to store food.

varieties (va-RYE-a-tees) - Different kinds of plants that are closely related.

Index